Enriching English 1

LANGUAGE COMPANION

Collins

Enriching English 1

LANGUAGE COMPANION

Published by Collins Learning
A division of HarperCollins*Publishers* India Private Limited
HarperCollins *Publishers*
A-75, Sector 57, Noida, Uttar Pradesh 201301, India
1 London Bridge Street, London, SE1 9GF, United Kingdom
2 Bloor Street East, Toronto, Ontario M4W 1A8, Canada
Lvl 13, 201 Elizabeth Street (PO Box A565, NSW, 1235), Sydney NSW 2000, Australia
195 Broadway, New York, NY 10007, USA

Browse the complete Collins catalogue at **www.collins.in**

First published in 2019

Reprint: 10 9 8 7 6 5 4 3 2 1

ISBN: 978-93-5277-995-6

Artwork and layout by QBS Learning
Cover layout by QBS Learning
Printed and bound by Nutech Print Services - India

FSC www.fsc.org MIX Paper from responsible sources FSC® C143748

This book is produced from independently certified FSC® paper to ensure responsible forest management.

Acknowledgements

The publishers would like to thank Aruna Punekar for contributing towards developing the content of *Enriching English Language Companion 1*.

The publishers have applied for permission for the following:

My Winter Friend from the website *Proud to be Primary (https://proudtobeprimary.com)*
Acknowledgement for the above will be made in the future editions of the book.

Cover: MashaStarus/iStockphoto.

Inside Page 34: Tera Vector; **38**: Exxorian; **39**: Blueringmedia; **51**: Tigatelu, Bandian1122, Bandian1122, LeeDaniels, Michelle_chen, Usagi-D, FancyTapis, Tigatelu; **68**: Svaga, AlfazetChronicles, Pijama61, Tigatelu, LPETTET, O-che; **69**: Tigatelu; **72**: Svaga, Malchev, Ekazansk, Pop_jop.

Preface

Literature as an area of study offers a unifying perspective of the world around us. It acts as a prism through which we can view every sphere of human civilization, including history and the sciences.

Enriching English is a language-through-literature course which is designed to introduce students to this larger world through a variety of literary works authored by Indian and global writers. In doing so, it also aims to build in students the foundations of English language by drawing their attention to the form and functions of language used in them.

The series comprises graded Readers and Language Companions, with support material in the form of Teacher's Resource Books and enhanced digital learning resources.

The **Readers** offer a wide variety of engaging literary texts organized thematically. Each unit in the Reader is built around a distinct theme, ranging from family and friendship, to wildlife and outer space. Besides teaching literary appreciation, each chapter in the Reader covers reading comprehension, vocabulary, grammar, listening, speaking, writing and study skills to help build language competency in students.

The **Language Companion** accompanying a reader aims to provide practice to the students in the same language skills and prepare them to excel in the *Language Paper* of the examination. For each thematic unit, extensive practice materials have been created with a special focus on developing reading comprehension, grammar and writing, following the pattern of the question paper used in the examination.

Each Language Companion is mapped to the Reader in two ways:

- It follows the themes covered in the Reader for the reading comprehension passages so that students have prior knowledge, and the context and vocabulary are in place to do the tasks given in the Language Companion independently.
- It covers the topic-wise language skills in the Reader sequentially and provides practice in each language item that needs to be mastered by the student.

To help students build a strong base in the use of correct tenses, a list of verb forms has been provided as appendix in books 3, 4 and 5.

We hope that teachers and parents will find this book useful in helping students practise and master English language to excel in the formal examinations that they are expected to take.

Detailed Contents

1 In the Park

Reading Comprehension

Read the passage carefully and answer the questions that follow.

Fun at the Park

On Sunday, Avi and his family visit a beautiful park. It is a place filled with trees, laughter and joy. There are many rides like slides, swings, see-saws and merry-go-rounds.

Avi and his sister, Ashi first enjoy the rides. They slide down the slide...WHOOOO. They swing on the swings....SWISH...SWISH. They go up and down the see-saw...TAY... TAY...TAY. They go round and round on the merry-go-round...GO...GO...GO.

In one corner of the park, in a small covered area, they see some white rabbits and some sweet little birds chirping. There is a small pond with many colourful fish in it. All around the pond are beautiful flowers and butterflies flying over them. Avi meets few friends in the park. They have also come with their parents. They have a lot of fun together. Their parents sit on the benches and enjoy the evening while watching them. They have ice cream, cotton candy and popcorn. By the end of the day, they are very tired, but happy. They all have a good time.

A. Fill in the blanks with words from the text.

1. Avi goes to a ________________ with his family.
2. He enjoys the rides with his ________________.
3. They go round and round on the ________________.
4. The rabbits are ________________ in colour.
5. Their parents sit on the ________________.

B. Answer these questions.

1. When and where does Avi go with his family?

   ____

   ____

2. What is the place filled with?

   ____

   ____

3. What do Avi and his sister do at first?

   ____

   ____

4. Who does Avi meet in the park?

   ____

   ____

5. What do they enjoy eating in the park?

   ____

   ____

C. Read the line and answer the questions.

By the end of the day, they are very tired, but happy.

1. Who is tired, but happy?

   ____

   ____

2. Why are they tired?

   ____

   ____

3. What makes them happy?

   ____

   ____

D. Name the following.

1. Three rides in the park

   ____________ ____________ ____________

2. Three animals in the park

   ____________ ____________ ____________

3. Three people in the park besides Avi

   ____________ ____________ ____________

4. Three things Avi ate in the park

   ____________ ____________ ____________

E. Use these words in sentences of your own.

1. visit ____________________
   ____
2. enjoy ____________________
   ____
3. tired ____________________
   ____

Vocabulary

Colours *Reader link: In the Park*

A. Match the pictures with their colours. Then colour the pictures.

1. yellow	a. 	b. 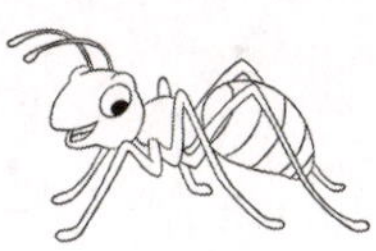	c. 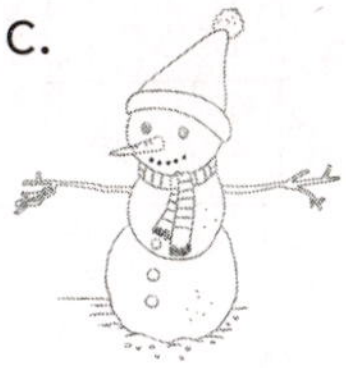	5. black
2. red	d. 	e. 		6. white
3. orange				7. blue
4. pink	f. 	g. 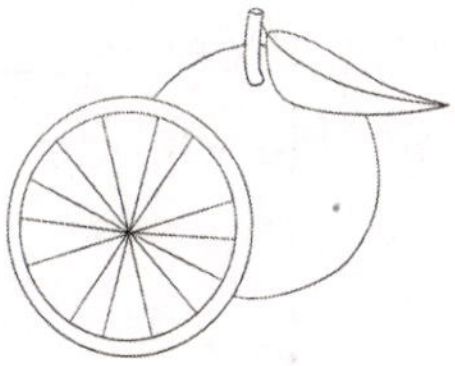	h. 	8. green

Feeling words *Reader link: In the Park*

B. Fill in the blanks with the correct feeling word.

angry happy tired afraid sad hungry

1. Jim is ____________ today. He won a prize at school.
2. Max looks ____________. He hasn't eaten anything since morning.
3. Ravi is ____________. He can't find his toy car.
4. The maid broke the flower vase. Mother is very ____________.
5. The children saw a snake in the garden. They are ____________.
6. Mother is ____________ after working for the whole day.

Rhyming words

Reader link: Swing, Swing, Swing

C. Write the name of the picture and match with the word it rhymes with.

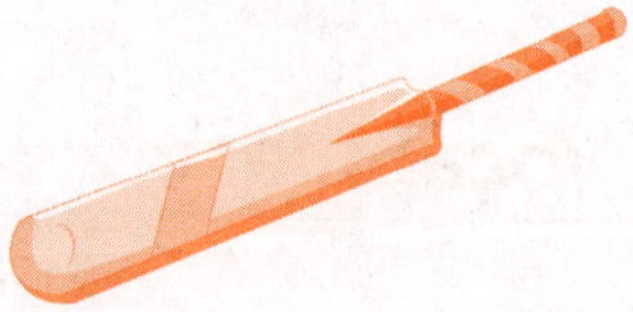

Opposite words

Reader link: Swing, Swing, Swing

D. Fill in the blanks with the opposite words of the words in bold.

1. A giraffe is **tall,** but a pony is ________________.
2. The table was **dirty**. We asked him to ________________ it.
3. Your clothes are ________________. Put them in the sun to **dry.**
4. I threw the ball **up** in the air. It came ________________ in no time.
5. My friend looks **sad** today. He will be ________________ if I play with him.

Grammar

Naming words

Reader link: In the Park

Naming words tell us the names of persons, places, animals or things.

Examples: Avi and his sister are persons. A rabbit is an animal.

A park is a place. An ice cream and a tree are things.

A. Read the passage again and underline all the naming words.

B. Read the passage given below and write down all the naming words in the table.

Mini is a new girl in the school. She is from a small town. Her pets are a sweet kitten and a talking parrot. She gives milk to her kitten and red chillies to her parrot. She loves to read storybooks. She also enjoys playing with her doll. Mini has made many friends. All the children play together in the park.

Person	Place	Animal	Thing

Study Skills

Spelling

Words with the same vowel

Reader link: In the Park

We know there are five vowels in the English alphabet.

They are ***a, e, i, o,*** and ***u.***

Write the word with the same vowel used in the words given below. Take help from the picture clues.

met: p ___ ___

small: b ___ ___ ___

dish: f___ ___ ___

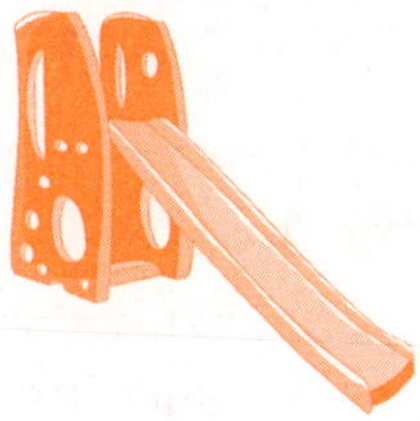

ride: ___ ___ ___ de

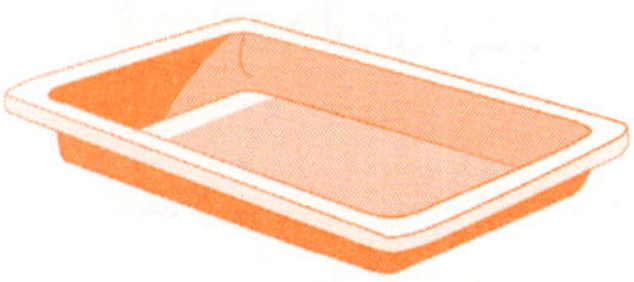

day: tr ___ ___

down: ___ ___ ___ wn

fun: ___ ___ n

ring: sw___ ___ ___

Listening

Listening for details

Reader link: In the Park

Listen and circle the words you hear.

In the summer, I like to go to the beach with my family. I splash in the water, and I jump up when a wave comes. I can only swim a little bit, but my father says I'm getting better. Something I love to do at the beach is play with my beach ball. I throw it in the water, and then I run and splash to get it out. I also like to dig into the sand with my spade and fill up my bucket. Then I tip the bucket over and make a sandcastle. I decorate the sandcastle with seashells.

Speaking

Talking about your favourite game

Reader link: In the Park

Speak about your favourite outdoor game. Take the help of these questions.

- What is your favourite outdoor game?
- Who do you play with?
- When do you play?
- How did you learn it?
- Who taught you to play the game?
- Who is your favourite player?

Writing

Writing about a park

Reader link: In the Park

A. Write about people and things you see at the park. Use the words given in the box.

balloons	balls	beautiful	benches	children	enjoy
flowers	grass	house	ice cream	parents	park
popcorn	sand-pit	slides	swings	trees	

Every Sunday I go to a ________________ with my younger sister and parents. It is not very far from my ________________. It is a ________________ place with so many shady ________________, colourful ________________ and green ________________. Many ________________ come with their ________________ to the park. There are many rides like ________________, ________________ and merry-go-rounds. There is also a ________________ for the children to play with sand. There are ________________ for people to sit. We get ________________ and ________________ outside the park. We can also find hawkers selling ________________ and ________________. The park is my favourite place where I ________________.

Picture composition

Reader link: In the Park

B. Look at the picture and complete the sentences.

having fun	are running	painting	is reading a book
in the park	swinging from the swing		

The children are playing ________________________________.

Two boys ________________________________.

One girl is ________________________________ and

another girl is ________________________ under the tree.

One boy ________________________________.

The children are ________________________________.

Activity

Colouring

Reader link: In the Park

Read and colour as directed.

- The cloud is grey.
- The tree is dark green and brown.
- The grass is light green.
- The fence is blue.
- The flowers are pink.
- The wall of the house is yellow.
- The windows of the house are blue.
- The chimney is red.
- The roof top and the door of the house are brown.

Now I can... Self-Assessment

- o read a passage and answer comprehension questions.
- o match pictures with their colours.
- o understand and use feeling words, rhyming words and opposite words.
- o understand and use naming words.
- o understand and use vowels.
- o listen to a passage and circle the correct words.
- o talk about my favourite game.
- o write about a park and complete a paragraph based on a picture.
- o colour a picture.

2 Celebrations

Reading Comprehension

Read the passage carefully and answer the questions that follow.

Annual Day

Today is our school's Annual Sports Day. There are many events throughout the day.

They are march pasts, relay races, hurdles, long and high jump. My class is in the march past.

I am taking part in the relay race. My best friend Avi is also in my relay race team. We have practised every day with the team. I hope our team wins the race. It will be great fun!

A. Fill in the blanks. Choose the correct option.

1. It is our Annual Sports Day ________________. (today/next week)
2. It is a ________________ event. (one-day/one-week)
3. My class is in the ________________. (dance/march past)
4. I am taking part in the ________________. (hurdle race/relay race)
5. Relay race is a ________________ event. (solo/team)

B. Answer these questions.

1. What is it today?

____

2. What all events are held throughout the day?

____

____

3. Which event is my class taking part in?

____

____

4. Who is in the relay race team?

____

____

5. Why do I hope my team wins the race?

____

____

C. Read the line and answer the questions.

I hope our team wins the race.

1. Which race do I hope to win?

____

2. Who are the team members?

____

3. When is the race going to be held?

____

Vocabulary

Words for food and drink *Reader link: Raha's Birthday*

A. Match the names with the pictures.

1. bread	a. 	7. egg	g. 
2. cake	b. 	8. biscuit	h. 
3. turnip	c. 	9. lemonade	i. 
4. soup	d. 	10. jam	j. 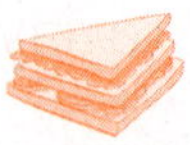
5. fish	e. 	11. sandwich	k. 
6. pear	f. 	12. carrot	l. 

B. Look at the pictures and write the names. Then write the two words each name is made of.

basketball	bathtub	doorbell	pancake	rainbow
sandcastle	snowman	starfish	sunflower	teapot

1.  basketball = basket + ball
2.  ________ = ________ + ________
3.  ________ = ________ + ________
4.  ________ = ________ + ________
5.  ________ = ________ + ________
6.  ________ = ________ + ________
7.  ________ = ________ + ________
8.  ________ = ________ + ________
9.  ________ = ________ + ________
10.  ________ = ________ + ________

Word meanings

Reader link: Springtime

C. Read the clues and choose the word from the box which means the same.

bouquet	balloon	celebrate	decorate
gather	gift	music	streamer

1. to enjoy an occasion: ____________
2. come together in a group: ____________
3. a bunch of flowers to be presented as a gift: ____________
4. something that you give someone, especially on a special occasion: ____________
5. the pattern of sounds produced by people singing or playing instruments: ____________
6. to make something look more attractive by putting things on it or around it: ____________
7. a brightly coloured thin rubber bag filled with air and used as a toy or decoration for parties: ____________
8. a long, narrow strip of brightly coloured paper used as a decoration for special occasions such as parties: ____________

Rhyming words

Reader link: Springtime

D. Circle the words that rhyme with the first word.

book	look	good	cook
fall	pole	call	ball
meet	eat	feet	head
play	clay	day	bye
coat	pot	boat	float
sun	fun	bun	hen
sing	king	bang	wing
fish	cash	dish	wish

Grammar

Common and special names *Reader link: Raha's Birthday*

We know that the names of persons, places, animals or things are called **naming words**. They can be **common** or **special**.

Common names tell us the general names used for people, places, animals and things.

Examples: boy, horse, school, bag

Special names tell us the particular name of a person, place, animal or thing. They always begin with a capital letter.

Examples: Gita, Delhi, Collins Dictionary

A. Circle the common names and underline the special names.

1. Ishan and Rishabh are twins.
2. I have a pet cat named Kitty.
3. Mr Gupta has bought a new car.
4. Ganga is the biggest river in India.
5. Did you burst crackers on Diwali?
6. We went to Goa in the summer holidays.
7. My father ordered a pizza from Pizza Plaza.
8. Sam had his birthday party on Saturday.

B. Fill in the blanks with special names.

My favourite...

- **cartoon character:** ____________
- **car:** ____________
- **city:** ____________
- **book:** ____________
- **player:** ____________
- **chocolate:** ____________

Naming words can be the names of one or more than one person, place, animal or thing. We add **-s** to a naming word to show more than one or many.

Example: one apple many apples

C. Write the naming words. Add -s to the naming words to show many.

1. __________ __________

2. __________ __________

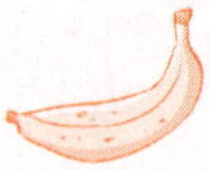

3. __________ __________

4. __________ __________

5. __________ __________

6. __________ __________

7. __________ __________

8. __________ __________

Study Skills

Spelling

Completing words with vowels *Reader link: Raha's Birthday*

Look at the pictures. Write the missing letters to complete the words.

1. B__ND

2. PR__S__NT

3. M__SIC

4. F__ __D

5. L__GHT__NG

6. D__NCE

7. C__PC__KE

8. PL__TES

9. FL__WERS

Listening

Listening for details *Reader link: Raha's Birthday*

Listen to a passage about a school carnival and circle the activities children enjoyed there.

Abracadabra	musical chair	Santa Claus
magic show	giant wheel	songs
crystal in the bowl	DJ point	horse ride
book stall	puppet show	Grandma Tales
lucky draw box	plum cakes	slides and swings

Speaking

Inviting someone

Reader link: Raha's Birthday

Work in pairs. Practise these dialogues with your partner. Invite him/her to a fancy dress party.

Writing

Making a list

Reader link: Raha's Birthday

A. Diwali, the festival of lights is one of the most important Hindu festivals. How will you celebrate Diwali this year? Complete the chart and plan for the festival. Help your mother make a list of the following:

- cleaning and decorating the house
- shopping – dresses, sweets, diyas, lights, gifts
- on the day of the celebration

cleaning and decorating the house

1. ______________________________
2. ______________________________
3. ______________________________

Shopping	Celebration
1. ______________________	1. ______________________
2. ______________________	2. ______________________
3. ______________________	3. ______________________

Picture composition

Reader link: Raha's Birthday

B. Look at the picture and complete the sentences. Use the words in the box.

sparkler	enjoying	rangoli	Diwali
decorated	family	happy	carrying

Riddhi is celebrating ______________ with her ______________ . The house is beautifully ______________ with a ______________ design at the entrance. Her mother is ______________ a tray of diyas. Her father is helping her to light the ______________ . Her elder brother is ______________ with her. All are looking very ______________ .

Now I can...

Self-Assessment

- read a passage and answer comprehension questions.
- match food and drink words with their pictures.
- understand and use compound words, word meanings and rhyming words.
- understand and use common and special names and the concept of one and many.
- complete words with vowels.
- listen to a passage and circle the correct words.
- invite someone to a fancy-dress party.
- make a list and complete a paragraph based on a picture.

3 Let Us Laugh

Reading Comprehension

Read the poem carefully and answer the questions that follow.

Chubby Little Snowman

A chubby little snowman
had a carrot nose.
Along came a rabbit
and what do you suppose?

That hungry little bunny
looking for his lunch
Ate the snowman's carrot nose...
Nibble, Nibble, Crunch!

A. Complete the sentences to write a summary.

1. There was a ______________ ______________ snowman.
2. He had a ______________ nose.
3. A hungry ______________ ______________ came along.
4. He was looking for ______________ ______________.
5. The rabbit ate ______________________________.

B. Answer these questions.

1. What kind of a snowman was he?

   ____

2. What was his nose made of?

   ____

3. What was the little bunny doing and why?

   ____

4. Did the bunny find food? How did he eat it?

____

5. What are the two pairs of rhyming words in the poem?

a. ____________________ b. ____________________

C. Give one word for:

1. plump and rounded ____________________
2. feeling the need for food ____________________
3. to eat or chew in small bits ____________________
4. model of a person made of snow ____________________

D. Complete the words with double consonants.

1. CHU__ __Y 2. CA__ __OT 3. LI__ __LE 4. BU__ __Y

Vocabulary

Shape words *Reader link: Catching Fish*

A. Write the shape of each object with the help of the given words.

square	triangle	oval	circle	rectangle

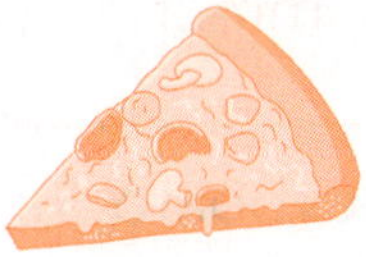

1. ____________________ 2. ____________________ 3. ____________________

4. ____________________ 5. ____________________

Sound words *Reader link: Catching Fish*

B. Fill in the blanks with the correct sound words.

beep crunch rumble chug

honk jingle chirp tick-tock

1. She heard the pennies ______________ in my pocket.
2. The ______________ of the clock kept me up all night.
3. I can hear the ______________ when my sister eats the cookies.
4. The cellphone gives a ______________ when the battery gets slow.
5. I like to hear the birds ______________ on my windowsill in the morning.
6. My pet dog hides under the bed when he hears the ______________ of thunder.
7. Rohan ran as fast as he could when he heard his school bus ______________.
8. I stood and watched as the train slowly ______________ out of the platform.

Word family *Reader link: Snowball*

C. Pick out a word that is different in each set. Say why you chose it.

1.	rose	lily	pink	lotus
2.	banana	pear	orange	cabbage
3.	table	basket	chair	bench
4.	winter	snow	summer	spring
5.	cellphone	mouse	keyboard	monitor
6.	eyes	ears	nose	legs
7.	pencil	eraser	nail clippers	ruler
8.	chess	football	cricket	basketball

Rhyming words *Reader link: Snowball*

D. Read the words in the box. Write the words with the same ending sounds inside the correct balls.

red	cap	hand	lip	bow	nose
skip	low	rose	band	tap	bed

________ ap

____

________ ed

____

________ ose

____

________ and

____

________ ow

____

________ ip

____

Grammar

Doing words

Reader link: Catching Fish

Doing words tell us what a person, animal or thing does.

Example: The sun **shines** brightly.

The mother bird **feeds** the baby birds.

A. Write the doing words for each picture.

1. ________

2. ________

3. ________

4. ________

write read clap
drink skip cook
drive kick watch pray

5. ________

6. ________

7. ________

8. ________

9. ________

10. ________

B. Fill in the blanks with the doing words given in the box.

sail	fly	love	wash	stand	cry	build	wear

1. My parents ________________ me.
2. Ships ________________ in the sea.
3. Kites ________________ high in the sky.
4. I always ________________ clean clothes.
5. They ________________ their car every Sunday.
6. Babies ________________ when they are hungry.

7. Children ________________ sandcastles on the beach.

8. We ________________ to attention for the national anthem.

Study Skills

Alphabetical order

Reader link: Catching Fish

Arrange these words in alphabetical order.

1. carrot snowman nose rabbit bunny lunch

____

2. little hungry crunch nibble chubby laugh

____

Listening

Listening for details

Reader link: Catching Fish

Listen carefully and complete the poem with the missing words.

My Winter Friend

One ____________ I went out to see
A world of ____________ in front of me.
So, I rolled three ____________
And stacked them up,
Rounded the sides
With a ____________ and a ____________.
I put on a top ____________,
A ____________ and a face.
I named my ____________ friend
And gave him an embrace.
I hope that you will ____________ for a while.
Oh ____________,
You have made me ____________!

Speaking

Asking and answering questions

Reader link: Catching Fish

Work in pairs. Ask and answer these questions about the things you do on Sunday.
Answer with 'Yes, I do.' or 'No, I don't.'

Do you go out with your family?

Do you help your parents in household chores?

Do you read a book on Sunday?

Writing

Picture composition

Reader link: Snowball

Complete the paragraph with the given words and find out how to build your own snowman.

snow	balls	stack	decorate	top	buttons
scarf	hat	enjoy	carrot	fun	twigs

How to build a snowman

First, make three ______________ of ______________.

______________ them on ______________ of each other.

Then, ______________ the snowman.

Use ______________ to make the eyes.

Take a ______________ to make the nose.

Next, use ______________ to make the limbs.

Finally, put on a ______________ at the top and a ______________ around the neck.

Now, ______________ with your snowman and have ______________.

Activity

Show and tell *Reader link: Snowball*

A. Work in pairs. Choose any one of these pictures. Describe them to your partner.

Circle time *Reader link: Snowball*

B. Sit in a circle. Each person tells a joke. Some are given here. You can share your own joke.

1. Teacher: Why are you late?
   Student: Because of the sign.
   Teacher: What sign?
   Student: The one that says, 'School Ahead, Go Slow.'
2. Mini: Mom, I think we need a new teacher.
   Mom: Why is that?
   Mini: Our teacher doesn't know anything. She keeps asking us for the answers.

Now I can... **Self-Assessment**

- o read a poem and answer comprehension questions.
- o understand and use shape words, sound words, word family and rhyming words.
- o understand and use doing words.
- o arrange words in alphabetical order.
- o listen to a poem and fill in the missing words.
- o ask and answer questions.
- o complete a paragraph based on a picture.
- o describe a picture and tell a joke.

4 Shopping

Reading Comprehension

Read the passage carefully and answer the questions that follow.

Santa's Workshop

Christmas is a very busy time for Santa and his elves at the North Pole. Santa's elves make the best toys in the world. These are made in Santa's workshop at the North Pole, also known as Lapland.

The 'workshop' is actually a huge complex with a factory, Santa's home, and a place for all his reindeers. The factory is where the elves make the toys and wrap them in colourful paper, so that Santa can distribute it to everyone on Christmas Eve.

A. Choose the correct option.

1. The busiest time for Santa and his elves is
   a. Diwali. b. Christmas. c. Holi.
2. Santa's workshop is at the
   a. Equator. b. South Pole. c. North Pole.
3. Santa's elves make toys in
   a. Santa's home. b. a factory. c. the Elves' home.
4. Santa's workshop also has a place for
   a. reindeers. b. horses. c. red foxes.
5. The toys are made so that
   a. the elves can play with them.
   b. Santa can distribute them on Christmas eve.
   c. the Christmas tree can be decorated with them.

B. Answer these questions.

1. Who is very busy on Christmas?
   ____
2. What are they busy doing?
   ____
3. What is Santa's workshop known as?
   ____
4. How are the toys packed after they are made?
   ____
5. When does Santa distribute the toys?
   ____

C. Read the lines and answer the questions.

These are made in Santa's workshop at the North Pole, also known as Lapland.

1. What is made in Santa's workshop?
   ____
2. Who makes them?
   ____
3. Why do they make them?
   ____

Vocabulary

Fruits and vegetables

Reader link: Rick Goes to the Market

A. Make a list of at least ten special things we buy at the supermarket or mall.

1. ______________
2. ______________
3. ______________
4. ______________
5. ______________
6. ______________
7. ______________
8. ______________
9. ______________
10. ______________

Names of places

Reader link: Rick Goes to the Market

B. Write the names of places we buy these things from.

1. pets ______________
2. books ______________
3. plants ______________
4. jewellery ______________
5. medicines ______________
6. cakes and pastries ______________
7. flowers and bouquets ______________
8. milk, butter and cheese ______________

Collocations: adjective-noun

Reader link: A Fairy Went a-Marketing

C. Join the words that go together.

1. bad	a. colour
2. best	b. day
3. bright	c. friend
4. deep	d. fun
5. great	e. habit
6. heavy	f. knife
7. rainy	g. sleep
8. sharp	h. wind
9. strong	i. traffic

Grammar

Describing words *Reader link: Rick Goes to the Market*

The words that tell us more about something or someone are called **describing words**.

Describing words tell us more about naming words.

Examples: colour pencil, beautiful tree, kind Santa

A. Underline the describing words.

1. It is a very hot day.
2. Monkeys have long tails.
3. Milk makes our bones strong.
4. I cleaned my dirty room yesterday.
5. Mani's naughty dog chewed my shoe.
6. We always buy fresh fruits and vegetables.
7. The cap seller slept in the cool shade of the tree.
8. My grandfather bought me a red bicycle on my birthday.

B. Fill in the blanks with the correct describing words.

black brave bright dirty hot red rich tiny

1. He is a very __________ soldier.
2. The clown had a __________ nose.
3. Hari washed his __________ hands.
4. A __________ spider crawled on the wall.
5. The __________ man lives in a big palace.
6. The __________ sun came out after the rain.
7. Tigers have __________ stripes on their body.
8. My mother gave me a glass of __________ milk to drink.

Punctuation: capital letters and full stop *Reader link: Rick Goes to the Market*

C. Rewrite these sentences using capital letters and full stops.

1. my birthday is in july

   ____

2. rohan is a smart boy

   ____

3. india is a big country

   ____

4. my sister is six years old

   ____

5. my cousin has a pet dog

   ____

6. the kitten plays with a ball

   ____

7. a sunflower is yellow in colour

   ____

8. children are playing in the garden

   ____

Study Skills

Pronunciation

Pronunciation: short and long *a* sounds *Reader link: Rick Goes to the Market*

Listen to the words and repeat them. Pay attention to the sound of *a* in them.

short *a*: ant bat cap hat jam pan mat van flag lamp
long *a*: bake day date face hare wake take plate snake table

Add three more words to each set.

short *a*: __________ __________ __________
long *a*: __________ __________ __________

Listening

Listening for details

Reader link: Rick Goes to the Market

Listen to the passage. Mark the sentences as true (T) or false (F).

1. My mother and I are in a shopping mall. ________
2. We first enter the supermarket. ________
3. I help my mother with the trolley. ________
4. My mother goes to the florist to buy flowers. ________
5. I buy two storybooks and some drawing sheets. ________
6. Feeling hot, we order an ice cream each. ________
7. In the cloth store, we buy some T-shirts and shorts. ________
8. After shopping, we come home by a taxi. ________

Speaking

Role play

Reader link: Rick Goes to the Market

Work with a partner. One of you can be the shopkeeper and the other can be the customer. Have a conversation with the shopkeeper. You can ask for what you need, make the payment, and say 'thank you'.

Writing

Paragraph writing

Reader link: Rick Goes to the Market

Look at the picture. Then answer the questions.

a rose plant	happy	with his father and sister
plant it in his garden	to buy plants	to the nursery

1. Where did Kunal go on Sunday?
2. Who went with him?
3. Why did they go there?
4. What did Kunal buy from there?
5. Is Kunal happy or sad?
6. What will Kunal do with it?

Now write the answers together, like a paragraph.

Activity

Playing a game

Reader link: A Fairy Went a-Marketing

Anna **Dia** **Firoz**

Let's play the alphabet shopping game.

Look at the picture.

Each child must name a thing they want to buy that begins with the first letter of their name.

Now I can... **Self-Assessment**

- read a passage and answer comprehension questions.
- make a list of fruits and vegetables, write names of places for shopping and understand and use adjective-noun collocations.
- understand and use describing words and punctuation.
- pronounce words with short and long *a* sounds.
- listen to a passage and write true or false.
- do a role play.
- write a paragraph based on a picture.
- play an alphabet shopping game.

5 Family

Reading Comprehension

Read the poem carefully and answer the questions that follow.

At the Zoo with Grandpa

Rony asked Grandpa,
'What shall we do?'
Grandpa said, 'It's a bright, sunny Sunday.
Let's go to the zoo!'
So, off they went with a camera
And a picnic lunch for two.

Grandpa drove to the zoo
Where they bought tickets for two.
Rony was happy and excited
So much so, that he shouted, 'Yippee! Yahoo!'

They saw lions, deer, bears,
Elephants, giraffes and kangaroos.
They also saw rare birds such as
Pink flamingos and bright cockatoos.
But what Rony loved best was
The gorilla, which shouted, 'Ha, ha! Hoo, hoo!'

A. Choose the correct option.

1. Rony and Grandpa went to the zoo on a
   a. Friday. b. Saturday. c. Sunday.
2. They took with them a
   a. mobile phone. b. camera and snacks. c. camera and a picnic lunch.
3. Who drove to the zoo?
   a. Grandpa b. Rony's father c. the driver
4. They bought tickets for
   a. two people. b. three people. c. four people.
5. The cockatoo is a
   a. wild animal. b. rare bird. c. water animal.
6. The animal Rony loved the best was the
   a. elephant. b. flamingo. c. gorilla.

B. Answer these questions.

1. What did Grandpa suggest Rony to do?
   ____
2. How was the weather that day?
   ____
3. How did they go to the zoo?
   ____
4. What was the first thing they did at the zoo?
   ____
5. Which animals and birds did they see at the zoo?
   ____
   ____

C. Read the lines and answer the questions.

Grandpa drove to the zoo
Where they bought tickets for two.
Ronny was happy and excited
So much so, that he shouted, 'Yippee! Yahoo!'

1. Where and when did Grandpa drive to?
   ____
2. Who did they buy the two tickets for?
   ____
3. How can you say that Rony was happy?
   ____
   ____

4. Give two rhyming words for 'Yahoo' from the lines.

a. ____________________ b. ____________________

Vocabulary

One word, two meanings *Reader link: Let Us Be Friends Again*

We know that the same word can have two different meanings. There are many such words that are fun to use, as they convey different meanings based on what we are talking about.

Examples: My mom kept the pickle in an airtight **can**. (a container)
She **can** ride a bicycle. (shows ability)

A. Here are some words which have more than one meaning. Match the words with their pictures.

1. 	a. band	i. 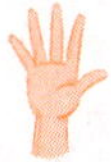
2. 	b. ring	ii. 
3. 	c. wave	iii. 
4. 	d. palm	iv. 

Words related to family *Reader link: Let Us Be Friends Again*

B. Fill in the blanks with the names of the family members.

father grandson granddaughter
aunt cousins sister nephew niece

This is Rohan's family. We can see Rohan with his mother and ____________, and his younger ____________, Ria.

His grandparents are also with them. Rohan and Ria are proud to be their ____________and ____________.

These are Rohan's uncle and ____________.
They have two children.
Rohan loves to play with his ____________.

This is Rohan's elder brother and his family.
They have twins – Ashi and Avi.
Ashi is Rohan's ____________ and Avi is Rohan's ____________.

Related words

Reader link: A Road Trip

C. Write down a word that relates to each of these words. Use the words given in the box.

rain	night	egg	green	trunk	candles	hot	time

1. moon ________

2. grass ________

3. umbrella ________

4. tea ________

5. elephant ________

6. hen ________

7. watch ____________

8. cake ____________

D. Label each group in the table with the correct name given in the box.

fruits	toys	tools	flowers	sports	insects

 rose lotus lily	 cricket football tennis	 teddy bear toy plane doll
1.	2.	3.
 ant butterfly honeybee	 apple mango pear	 hammer screwdriver saw
4.	5.	6.

Grammar

Prepositions

Reader link: Let Us Be Friends Again

A **preposition** tells us where a person, animal, place or thing is.

It tells us the position of something.

Examples: The rabbit is

in the hat. **on** the table. **under** the table.

A. Underline the prepositions in these sentences.

1. I looked under my bed.
2. The chair is beside the table.
3. The book kept on the table is mine.
4. The plane was flying above the clouds.
5. There are some apples in the fruit bowl.
6. The girl looked behind the door for her friend who was hiding there.

B. Look at the picture. Fill in the blanks with the correct prepositions from the box.

up	on	under	above	in	beside	behind

1. The cat is sitting ________ the treehouse.
2. The boy is climbing ________ the ladder.
3. The birds are flying ________ the tree.
4. We can see some mushrooms growing ________ the tree.
5. The little squirrel is ________ its hole.
6. There is a bell hanging ________ the girl.
7. We can see some green bushes ________ the tree.

This and that

Reader link: Let Us Be Friends Again

This and **that** point to people, places, and objects.

This is used for things which are **nearby**.

That is used for things which are **far** from us.

Both **this** and **that** are used for singular naming words.

C. Fill in the blanks with *this* or *that*.

1. ________ book is very interesting.

2. ________ car is moving at great speed.

3. ________ kite has a colourful tail.

4. ________ boy needs help.

5. ________ child is not well.

6. ________ castle is very old.

Doing words with *-ing*

Reader link: Let Us Be Friends Again

We have learnt that ***-ing*** is added at the end of doing words to show an action that is going on at the time of speaking. We use these doing words with ***is, am,*** or ***are***.

Examples:

The bird **is singing.**

The children **are playing.**

D. Fill in the blanks with the correct words from the box. Add *-ing* to the word and use it with *am, is* or *are.*

build	write	bark	wait	cry	go	swim	rain

1. We ________________ for a picnic.
2. Children ________________ in the pool.
3. The baby ________________ as it is hungry.
4. She ________________ a letter to her friend.
5. I ________________ for the bus with my friend.
6. It ________________. Take your umbrella with you.
7. They ________________ a sandcastle on the beach.
8. The dog ________________. There is someone outside.

Pronouns

Reader link: A Road Trip

Pronouns are words which are used in the place of nouns or naming words.

Examples: It is **Harsh**'s birthday. **Harsh** is very happy today.
It is **Harsh**'s birthday. **He** is very happy today.
The **boys** played well. **The boys** won the match.
The **boys** played well. **They** won the match.

He and ***they*** are pronouns.

E. Fill in the blanks with *he, she, it,* or *they.*

1. Raghu is crying. ________ lost his new ball.
2. I cannot carry my bag. ________ is too heavy.
3. Naisha loves to dance. ________ is a good dancer.
4. Your dress is so beautiful. When did you buy ________?
5. I have a pet cat and a dog. ________ are my good friends.
6. Darsh is not well. ________ has not come to school today.
7. Tiya and Navya are friends. ________ study in the same class.
8. My grandma knows many stories. ________ tells me one story every night.

Study Skills

Spelling

Reader link: Let Us Be Friends Again

Look at the pictures and words below them. Tick the correct spelling.

 tabel table tebel	 shose soose shoes	 fairy feary ferry	 leef leif leaf
 goat gote gaot	 hause house haose	 milk mlik milik	 brid bird bud

Listening

Listening to and solving riddles

Reader link: A Road Trip

Listen to the riddles and write the answers.

1. I am a silver ball,
   Not found in the mall. You see me at night
   I take the place of the sun so bright
   I am the ____________________.

2. I am black and grey, With small eyes and a long tail
   I run in the fields eating grain
   And hide in the hole in the rain.
   I am a ____________________.

3. I am black and yellow and Fly on the flowers—high and low. I suck its juice and make a sweet, And give the bear a lovely treat.
   I am a ____________________.

4. I am thin, I am fat,
   In your bags, on the shelves—
   Full of kings, queens, fairies and elves!
   I am your best friend till the end
   I am a ____________________.

5. I am big, I am small. I give many things to all. Birds live on me, mice live under me
   Let me live, please don't cut me.
   I am a ____________________.

6. I have no colour.
   Without me, everyone will suffer.
   I make your food, and your tea;
   I am in the river and the sea.
   I am ____________________.

Speaking

Talking about your family *Reader link: Let Us Be Friends Again*

A. Work in pairs. Tell your friends about your family. You may say:

I live in a big/small family. There are __________ members in the family. My father is a __________. My mother is a __________. I have a sister/brother. He/She is __________ years old and studies in Class __________. I love to play with __________. My grandfather and grandmother stay with us. They love me very much. I too love them.

B. Similarly, you can speak about your uncle, aunt and cousins.

Writing

Simple sentences *Reader link: Let Us Be Friends Again*

Put these words in the correct order to form sentences.

1. village. / My / live / in / a / grandparents

   ____

2. uncle / aunt / My / stay / them. / and / with / also

   ____

3. summer / year / holidays / spent / I / them. / with / Last / my

   ____

4. delicious / cooked / many / things / grandmother / My / me. / for

   ____

5. swimming. / My / taught / uncle / me

   ____

6. time / had / We / good / together. / a

   ____

Now I can... **Self-Assessment**

- read a poem and answer comprehension questions.
- identify one word with two meanings, words related to family, and related words.
- use prepositions, *this* and *that*, doing words with *-ing* and pronouns.
- identify the correct spellings.
- listen to and solve riddles, and talk about my family.
- write simple sentences.

6 Folktales

Reading Comprehension

Read the passage carefully and answer the questions that follow.

The Wind and the Sun

One day, the Wind and the Sun were fighting. Each said that he was stronger than the other. Suddenly, they saw a traveller walking down the road. The Sun said, 'I see a way to end our fight. He who can make that traveller take off his cloak shall be considered stronger. You begin.'

The Sun hid behind a cloud. The Wind began to blow as hard as he could. But the harder he blew, the more tightly the traveller wrapped his cloak around him. The Wind finally gave up.

Then, the Sun came out and shone brightly. The traveller found it too hot to walk with his cloak on. So, he took it off.

A. Arrange the sentences in the correct order.

☐ They saw a traveller walking down the road.

☐ When the traveller felt too hot, he took off his cloak.

☐ The Wind and the Sun were fighting about who was stronger.

☐ The Sun came out and shone brightly.

☐ The Wind began to blow as hard as it could.

B. Answer these questions.

1. Why were the Wind and the Sun fighting?

____

____

2. What way did they find to end their fight?

____

____

3. What happened when the Wind began to blow hard?

____

____

4. How did the Sun make the traveller take off his cloak?

____

____

C. Read the lines and answer the questions.

'I see a way to end our fight. He who can make that traveller take off his cloak shall be considered stronger. You begin.'

1. Who said these words to whom?

____

2. What was the fight about?

____

____

3. Who was stronger in the end?

____

____

D. Match the words with their meanings.

Word	Meaning
1. cloak	a. great beauty
2. glory	b. unkind or cruel
3. harsh	c. a person who is on a journey
4. wrap	d. a long loose coat without sleeves
5. traveller	e. to cover something with paper, cloth or other material

Vocabulary

Animal sounds

Reader link: The Lion and the Hare

A. All animals make different sounds. Look at the pictures, and write the sounds these animals make. Use words from the box.

squeak	hiss	buzz	croak	hoot	roar	chatter	bleat	howl

1. 
2. 
3. 
4. 
5. 
6. 
7. 
8. 
9. 

Opposite words

Reader link: The Lion and the Hare

B. Write the opposites of these words.

1. hard ______________
2. hot ______________
3. in ______________
4. lose ______________
5. on ______________
6. start ______________
7. strong ______________
8. up ______________

Animal homes

Reader link: The Little Red Hen

C. We know that different animals live in different homes. Fill in the blanks with the words given in the box.

pen	tree	web	den	hole	kennel	pond	nest

1. A lion lives in a ______________.
2. A bird lives in a ______________.
3. A frog lives in a ______________.
4. A spider lives in a ______________.
5. A dog lives in a ______________ and a sheep lives in a ______________.
6. A rat lives in a ______________ while a monkey lives on a ______________.

Grammar

Future tense

Reader link: The Lion and the Hare

When we talk about an action which is going to happen at a time later than now, we add **will** before a doing word.

Examples: I **will go** to the market in the evening.
My friends **will come** to my house today.

The word **will** in these sentences tells us what is going to happen later.

A. Fill in the blanks with the correct form of the doing words given in the brackets.

1. The sky is full of dark clouds. It ________________. (rain)
2. I ________________ reading the book by evening. (finish)
3. He ________________ his homework after his dinner. (do)
4. We ________________ Agra during our hoildays. (visit)
5. My parents ________________ a new house next year. (buy)
6. The parrot ________________ away if you disturb it. (fly)
7. My mother ________________ pizza for me tomorrow. (make)
8. Eat something or you ________________ hungry on the way. (be)

Using *not*

Reader link: The Lion and the Hare

B. We can make negative sentences by adding *not*. Change these sentences using *not*.

1. He is tired.

   ____

2. His room is clean.

   ____

3. He will play with me.

   ____

4. The cat will drink the milk.

   ____

5. My brother is very naughty.

   ____

6. My father will buy me a new toy.

____

7. My friend was angry with me.

____

8. We are going for a movie.

____

Joining words: *and, or, but* *Reader link: The Little Red Hen*

Words like **and**, **but** and **or** are used to join words, sentences or parts of sentences together. They are called **joining words**.

C. Fill in the blanks with the correct joining words.

1. Will you watch TV ______________ read a book?
2. Is Rishi your brother ______________ your cousin?
3. Nitya works hard ______________ her brother is lazy.
4. I rang the bell ______________ no one opened the door.
5. You must not tell lies ______________ your mother will be angry.
6. She bought some fruits ______________ vegetables from the market.
7. I like to go for a walk ______________ getting up early is very difficult.
8. My grandmother took me to the shop ______________ bought me a new dress.

Describing words *Reader link: The Little Red Hen*

D. Read the paragraph, and circle the describing words in it.

One sunny day, my little puppy jumped onto my soft bed and played with a new ball. It was fun watching the cute puppy playing. Soon, it was tired and looked at me with sad eyes. I gave it warm milk and bread in a small bowl. It was happy and wagged its short, fluffy tail.

Study Skills

Pronunciation *Reader link: The Lion and the Hare*

A. Listen and repeat. Then, place the words in the correct column as per the sound.

egg pea tree gem seal queen hen feet red meat den

e sound	ea/ee sound
______	______
______	______
______	______
______	______
______	______
______	______

Spelling *Reader link: The Little Red Hen*

B. Unscramble the words.

1. 
SNTE
______

2. 
REBA
______

3. 
FTIRU
______

4. 
DCUOL
______

5. 
HOES
______

6. 
IRFE
______

7. 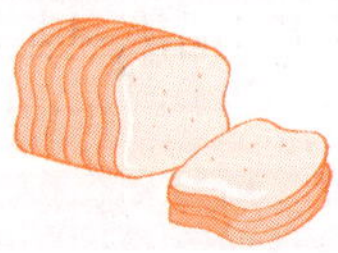
REBDA
______

8. 
RHIST
______

Listening

Listening for details *Reader link: The Lion and the Hare*

Listen to the story, and complete these sentences.

One day, Bonny Bear was feeling very ______________. So, she went out of her ______________ in search of food.

Bonny Bear went to the river to catch some ______________. She stood by the river and saw lots of fish in it. She was very happy and she was able to catch one. But then, the Bonnie Bear thought, 'This is such a ______________ fish to fill my stomach. I must catch a ______________ fish.' So, she let the small fish go and waited for a big fish to come by. Then again a small fish came and she let it go thinking that the small fish would not fill her ______________. This way she caught many small fish, but let all of them go off.

By ______________, the Bonny Bear had not caught any big fish. She slowly began to feel ______________. At the end of the day, she remained ______________ and thought, 'All those small fish, together would have filled up my belly, but now it was too ______________.'

Moral of the story: A small fish in hand is worth a big fish in the water.

Speaking

Thanking someone *Reader link: The Lion and the Hare*

Read how Sheeba thanks her teacher Ms Meera for helping her prepare for the dance competition.

Sheeba: Good morning, Ms Meera. How are you?

Ms Meera: I'm good, dear. Congratulations for winning the first prize in the Dance Competition.

Sheeba: Thank you for helping me, Miss.

Now think of an incident when your family member helped you. Thank him/her.

Tell him/her why you are thankful.

You may thank the family member for:

- organising your birthday party
- helping you with your homework
- caring for you when you were not well

Writing

Sequencing and writing a story

Reader link: The Lion and the Hare

A. Read these sentences. Then, number them in the correct order to find out what a clever fox does to come out of the well he fell into. Rewrite the story in your notebook.

☐ The fox slipped and fell into the well.
☐ The foolish goat also jumped into the well.
☐ He tried to come out. But he could not do so.
☐ After some time, there came a goat who was also thirsty.
☐ Once, a thirsty fox saw a big well nearby and peeped into it.
☐ The clever fox climbed on the back of the goat and jumped out of the well.
☐ The fox saw the goat and said loudly from inside the well, 'The water is very sweet. Come and enjoy.'

B. Which of the two characters in the above story do you like the most? Why? Use the words given in the box to fill in the table.

clever	gentle	polite	strong	harsh	foolish

The character I like the most is ____________________

My first reason is:	My second reason is:
____________________	____________________
____________________	____________________
____________________	____________________
____________________	____________________
____________________	____________________

Now I can... **Self-Assessment**

- read a passage and answer comprehension questions.
- identify animal sounds and homes, and write opposite words.
- understand and use the future tense, *not* in negative sentences, joining words and describing words.
- pronounce words with *e* and *ea*/*ee* sounds and unscramble words.
- listen to a short story and fill in the blanks, and thank someone.
- write a story in the correct sequence of events.

7 Holidays

Reading Comprehension

Read the passage carefully and answer the questions that follow.

I am going to Goa for a week with my family. We are going to stay with my uncle. My uncle lives in Panjim. His house is near the Miramar Beach.

I will be meeting my cousin. She is seven years old. She is learning to play the piano. We will play at the beach every day.

I want to search for seashells on the beach. I want to make a necklace of the seashells and give it to my grandma on her birthday.

A. State whether the following sentences are true (T) or False (F).

1. The child is going to Goa for a month. ☐
2. He is going to stay in a hotel. ☐
3. The child's uncle has a house near the beach. ☐
4. The child has a cousin who is learning to play the guitar. ☐
5. The child wants to gift a seashell necklace to his grandma on her birthday. ☐

B. Answer these questions.

1. Where is the child going with his family?

____

____

2. Where are they going to stay?

____

____

3. Where does the child's uncle live?

____

____

4. Who will the child play with?

____

____

5. What does the child want to do on the beach besides playing?

____

____

6. What does he want to gift his grandma on her birthday?

____

____

C. Read the line and answer the questions.

I want to search for seashells on the beach.

1. Where is the beach?

____

2. Who wants to search for the seashells?

____

3. What does he want to do with the seashells?

____

Vocabulary

Weather words

Reader link: Nida's Adventure

A. Underline the weather words.

1. Take an umbrella. It is raining.
2. It is too windy to play badminton today.
3. Look! There is a beautiful rainbow in the sky.
4. We could not see the bridge because of the fog.
5. I could not sleep because the thunder was too loud.
6. It is a bit chilly today. So, I think you should wear a coat.
7. The weather is very hot. Let us go for a swim in the lake.
8. We hope to have sunshine on the day of the beach picnic.

Names of months *Reader link: Picnic at the Beach*

B. Look at the pictures and name the months.

1. ____________

2. ____________

3. ____________

4. ____________

5. ____________

6. ____________

7. ____________

8. ____________

9. ____________

Grammar

Using verbs

Reader link: Nida's Adventure

We have learnt that ***am, is, are, has, have, do*** and ***does*** are verbs. Here is how we use them:

I	am/have
He/She (one person)	is/has/does (verbs ending with 's')
You/We/They (more than one person)	are/do/have (verbs not ending with 's')

A. Circle the correct verb in each sentence.

1. Soham ______________ (is/are) my best friend.
2. I ______________ (am/is) not feeling well today.
3. I ______________(have/has) to do my homework.
4. He ______________ (is/are) a good cricket player.
5. They ______________ (has/have) bought a new car.
6. She ______________ (do/does) her work very neatly.
7. I know you ______________ (do/does) not like the rains.
8. Meera and Esha ______________ (has/have) gone to the party.

B. Rewrite the sentences correctly.

1. She have a pet cat.

   ____

2. He do not drink tea.

   ____

3. You am late for the class.

   ____

4. The children does their work quietly.

   ____

5. They has many flowers in their garden.

   ____

6. My father are going to Delhi tomorrow.

   ____

7. We has a dance competition next week.

   ____

8. Tina and Manya is coming for the picnic with us.

   ____

Study Skills

Pronunciation

Short and long sounds of 'i' *Reader link: Nida's Adventure*

Say these words aloud. Pay attention to the sound of *i* in them.

short i: in his sit big dip fill give king milk ship

long i: ice lie high five pine wide knife light smile

Listening

Listening for details *Reader link: Nida's Adventure*

Listen how Alia enjoyed her holidays. Then, mark the sentences as true (T) or false (F).

1. Alia has a month-long winter vacation. ☐
2. She does lot of household work. ☐
3. They go to their grandparents' house on a hill station. ☐
4. They fly kites with their grandfather. ☐
5. Alia plays with the cows. ☐
6. Their grandmother tells them stories of her childhood days. ☐

Speaking

Role-playing a conversation *Reader link: Nida's Adventure*

Work in groups of four. Each student in the group will play the role of mother, father, you and your sister. Talk to your family members about where they wish to go for the holidays. You may begin like this...

You: Mother, the summer holidays are beginning from 1st May. We can go to Goa. I love playing on the beach. We can make sandcastles. What do you think?

Mother: No, I think this year we should go to a hill station.

You: Didi, what do you say?

Sister: No, I want to go to an adventure camp.

You: Didi, I know it's fun. But we went to an adventure camp last year also.
Sister: But all my friends are going. I don't want to miss it.
Mom: Let's talk to Father. I'm sure he must have planned something.

Writing

Picture composition *Reader link: Nida's Adventure*

Look at the picture and complete the sentences. Use the words in the box.

bicycle	doll	green	park	baby	slide
book	enjoying	bench			

1. This is a beautiful ________________, covered with ________________ grass.
2. Two women are sitting on the ________________.
3. One woman is holding her ________________ in her hand.
4. The other woman is reading a ________________.

5. Two friends are fighting for a ________________.

6. A little boy is playing on the ________________.

7. A ________________ is lying on the path.

8. A dog is also ________________ in the park.

Activity

Holiday hobby *Reader link: Picnic at the Beach*

What do you like to do during your holidays? Do you collect shells or small local artefacts when you are on a holiday? Talk about it in class. You can talk about the following:

- What is it?
- Where did you get it from?
- How much did it cost?
- What is it made of?
- Why is it so important?

Now I can... **Self-Assessment**

- o read a passage and answer comprehension questions.
- o identify the correct weather words and names of months.
- o understand and use verbs.
- o pronounce words with short and long *i* sounds.
- o listen to a passage and identify statements as true or false.
- o role-play a conversation.
- o complete sentences based on a picture.
- o write about my holiday hobby.

8 Animal Stories

Reading Comprehension

Read the passage carefully and answer the questions that follow.

Once there was a fox. His neighbour was a stork. The fox used to always laugh at the way the stork looked. One day, he thought of a plan to have some fun. He invited the stork to dinner. The stork gladly accepted the invitation.

For dinner, the fox served soup in a plate. The stork could not have the soup from the plate with his long beak. The hungry stork was angry at the fox but did not show his anger. Instead, he invited the fox to dine with him, in turn.

The next day, the fox arrived on time at the stork's house. The stork served soup in a tall jar with a very long neck. The stork could easily eat with his long beak. But the fox could only lick the outside of the jar. Soon the fox got very angry at the stork. The stork said, 'Do not play tricks on your neighbours unless you can stand the same treatment yourself.'

A. Match the parts to complete the sentences.

Column A	Column B
1. The fox used to always laugh	a. with his long beak.
2. To have some fun, the fox	b. tricks on our neighbours.
3. The stork could not have the soup from the plate	c. at the way the stork looked.
4. The hungry stork was angry at the fox	d. in a tall jar with a very long neck.
5. The stork served the soup	e. invited the stork to dinner.
6. We should not play	f. but did not show his anger.

B. Answer these questions.

1. Who did the fox laugh at and why?

2. Why couldn't the stork have the soup?

3. How did the stork serve the soup to the fox?

4. Could the fox have the soup?

5. What did the stork say to the fox?

C. Read the lines and answer the questions.

1. *He invited the stork to dinner.*
   a. Who invited the stork to dinner?

   b. What did he serve the stork?

   c. Was the stork able to enjoy his dinner? Why?

2. *The next day, the fox arrived on time at the stork's house.*
   a. Why did the fox come to the stork's house?

   b. How did the stork welcome his guest?

   c. Was the fox happy with the stork?

Vocabulary

Jobs

Reader link: The Fox and the Bear

We know that there are many people in our daily life who help us in getting things done.

They do various **jobs**.

Examples: teacher, baker, pilot, gardener

A. Look at the pictures. Match the pictures with the words given in the box.

policeman	fireman	cobbler	plumber	electrician	nurse
mechanic	farmer	mason	lifeguard	bus driver	sweeper

1. ____________

2. ____________

3. ____________

4. ____________

5. ____________

6. ____________

7. ____________________

8. ____________________

9. ____________________

10. ____________________

11. ____________________

12. ____________________

Ordinal and cardinal numbers

Reader link: The Fox and the Bear

One, two, three are **cardinal** numbers.

First, second, third are **ordinal** numbers.

B. Look at the picture. The animals are running a race. Can you tell the position of each animal?

1. The elephant is the winner. He is ____________ in the race.
2. The zebra is at the ____________ position.
3. The horse is at the ____________ position, but he is running very fast to beat the other animals.
4. The giraffe with his long steps is at the ____________ position.
5. The ____________ is running behind the giraffe and is at the ____________ position.
6. The bear with his tiny steps can be seen running at the ____________ position.

Animal movement words *Reader link: Creepy Crawly*

C. We know that different animals move in different ways. Some hop and jump, while others slither and swim. Fill in the blanks with the movement words from the box.

runs	flutters	climbs	prowls	waddles	crawls	gallops	glides

1. A duck ____________.

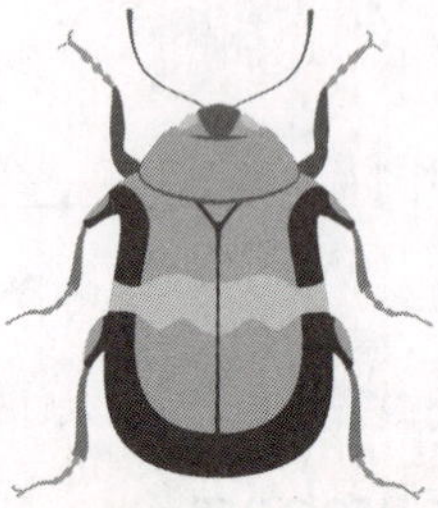

2. A beetle ____________.

3. A dog ____________.

4. A monkey ____________.

5. A butterfly ____________.

6. A seagull ____________.

7. A lion ___________.

8. A horse ___________.

Grammar

Possessives

Reader link: The Fox and the Bear

We have learnt that the words like **your, my, his, their** and **our** show that something belongs to someone.

Examples: **My** bag

His book

Their house

A. Fill in the blanks with the correct words from the box.

his	our	her	its	their	our

1. Tina is playing with ______________ doll.
2. The dog is happy. It is wagging ______________ tail.
3. We are Indians. We are proud of ______________ country.
4. They have bought a new car. ______________ car is red in colour.
5. We are waiting for ______________ friend. We are going to a party.
6. Ali is reading a book that ______________ aunt gave him on his birthday.

A and an *Reader link: The Fox and the Bear*

A and **an** are used with singular naming words.

We write **a** before naming words that begin with consonants.

Examples: a horse, **a** pen

We write **an** before naming words that begin with any of the five vowels: a, e, i, o and u.

Examples: an owl, **an** elephant

B. Fill in the blanks with *a* or *an*.

1. Today is ________ hot day.
2. Let us read ________ story.
3. We saw ________ white tiger at the zoo.
4. I have ________ egg for breakfast every day.
5. I saw ________ owl sitting on a tree in my garden.
6. There is ________ glass of milk for you on the table.
7. She took ________ umbrella with her, as it was raining.
8. I bought ________ ice cream for myself and ________ chocolate for my little brother.

Study Skills

Alphabetical order *Reader link: The Fox and the Bear*

Arrange these words from the story in alphabetical order.

fox stork plan dinner fun house beak soup jar trick

____

____

Listening

Listening for details

Reader link: The Fox and the Bear

Listen to the fox facts and tick the correct option.

1. The fox is the member of the **cat/dog** family.
2. Their **eyes/ears** are like a cat.
3. The foxes hunt like a **cat/lion**.
4. A fox's home is called a **cave/den**.
5. The foxes eat **fruits/small animals**.
6. Foxes can steal **chickens/puppies** from a house.
7. A female fox is called **foxy/vixen**.
8. A baby fox is called a **cub/calf**.

Speaking

These and those

Reader link: The Fox and the Bear

This and **these** are used for things near us.

That and **those** are used for things far away from us.

Now, look at this table.

	Singular	**Plural**
Near	this	these
Far	that	those

Work in pairs. Look at the pictures and ask questions. Then, answer them using *this/that is* or *these/those are*.

	What is this/are these?   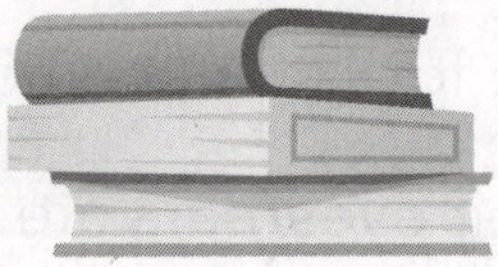
	What is that/are those?   

Writing

Rebus story *Reader link: The Fox and the Bear*

A. Read and complete this story. Write down the correct words for all the pictures.

One day, the  ________ was shining. A  ________ was swinging

from a  ________. An  ________ lived in the same  ________.

It was trying to sleep. But a  ________ who lived in the  ________

nearby was croaking loudly. It had seen a  ________.

'Help! Help!' it croaked.

The  ________ chattered loudly and climbed higher up the  ________.

The  ________ screeched loudly and tried to sleep through the commotion.

The  ________ jumped out of the  ________ and hopped away.

The  ________ hissed and glided away and the  ________ went on shining.

B. Write a paragraph on your favourite animal. Write about the following:

- How does it look – size and colour?
- Where does it live?
- What does it eat?
- What is its baby called?
- Why do you like it?

Activity

Charades

Take turns to act like an animal, while the other children try to identify the animal.

Now I can...

Self-Assessment

- o read a passage and answer comprehension questions.
- o identify different jobs, understand and use ordinal and cardinal numbers, and identify animal movement words.
- o understand and use possessives and *a* and *an*.
- o arrange words in alphabetical order.
- o listen to a passage and choose the correct option.
- o understand and use *these* and *those*.
- o complete a rebus story and write a paragraph on my favourite animal.
- o play charades by pretending to be an animal.

Common Words to Know and Spell

Here's a list of common words used in English. Learn to spell them.

a	black	could	fall	girl	home	let	move	own	saw
about	blue	cow	far	give	hop	light	much	page	say
add	boat	cry	farm	glad	hope	like	must	pan	school
after	book	cup	fast	go	horse	line	my	park	sea
ago	both	cut	fat	goat	hot	little	myself	part	seat
all	box	dad	father	goes	house	live	nail	pay	see
am	boy	daddy	feed	going	how	lives	name	pet	seem
an	bring	day	feel	gold	hurt	long	need	pick	seen
and	brother	dear	feet	gone	I	look	never	plant	send
any	brown	deep	fell	good	ice	looking	new	play	set
apple	bus	deer	find	got	if	lost	next	playing	seven
are	but	did	fire	grass	in	lot	nice	pony	she
as	buy	do	first	green	inside	love	night	post	sheep
ask	by	dog	fish	grow	into	mad	nine	pull	ship
at	cake	doing	five	had	is	made	no	put	shoe
ate	call	doll	fix	hand	it	make	not	rabbit	show
away	came	done	flag	happy	its	man	now	rain	sick
baby	can	door	floor	hard	job	many	nut	ran	side
back	candy	down	fly	has	jump	may	of	rat	sing
bad	car	draw	food	hat	just	me	off	read	sit
ball	carry	dress	foot	have	keep	meat	oh	red	six
bat	cat	drink	for	he	kind	men	old	rest	sky
be	change	drive	four	hear	king	met	on	ride	sleep
bed	child	drop	fox	help	know	mile	one	riding	small
bee	city	dry	from	hen	lake	milk	only	road	snow
been	class	duck	full	here	land	mine	open	rock	so
before	clean	each	fun	hill	last	miss	or	room	some
best	coat	eat	funny	him	late	mom	other	run	soon
better	cold	eating	game	his	laugh	moon	our	said	spell
big	come	egg	gas	hit	lay	more	out	same	start
bike	coming	eight	gave	hold	left	most	outside	sang	stay
bird	corn	end	get	hole	leg	mother	over	sat	still

stop	tell	there	today	tree	walk	well	why	yellow
store	ten	they	together	truck	want	went	will	yes
story	than	thing	told	try	warm	were	wind	yet
sun	thank	think	too	two	was	wet	wish	you
take	that	this	took	up	wash	what	with	your
talk	the	three	top	us	way	when	woke	zoo
tall	them	time	toy	use	we	while	wood	
teach	then	to	train	very	week	who	work	

Singular and Plural Nouns

Here is a list of noun forms for you to know.

Words with *-s*

Singular	Plural	Singular	Plural
park	parks	balloon	balloons
swing	swings	week	weeks
sister	sisters	cousin	cousins
corner	corners	year	years
rabbit	rabbits	piano	pianos
bird	birds	shell	shells
pond	ponds	sea	seas
flower	flowers	birthday	birthdays
friend	friends	neighbour	neighbours
day	days	stork	storks
school	schools	pet	pets
event	events	soup	soups
team	teams	beak	beaks
carrot	carrots	jar	jars
toy	toys	neck	necks
shop	shops	trick	tricks
reindeer	reindeers	cat	cats
paper	papers	manner	manners
zoo	zoos	fool	fools
camera	cameras	dog	dogs
picnic	picnics	sack	sacks
ticket	tickets	hunter	hunters
lion	lions	top	tops
bear	bears	mouth	mouths
elephant	elephants	pillow	pillows
kangaroo	kangaroos	flight	flights
gorilla	gorillas	room	rooms
wind	winds	wing	wings
traveller	travellers	thing	things
road	roads	bowl	bowls
fight	fights	pea	peas
cloak	cloaks	door	doors
cloud	clouds	garden	gardens
paper	papers	plant	plants

Singular	Plural	Singular	Plural
tail	tails	ocean	oceans
crown	crowns	thought	thoughts
brother	brothers	farmer	farmers
gift	gifts	field	fields
girl	girls	sparrow	sparrows
idea	ideas	nest	nests
flag	flags	season	seasons
way	ways	word	words
card	cards	relative	relatives
track	tracks	animal	animals
fin	fins	forest	forests